A
MINIATURE
CATHEDRAL
AND OTHER POEMS

A MINIATURE CATHEDRAL

AND OTHER POEMS

WALTER WANGERIN, JR.

1817

HARPER & ROW, PUBLISHERS, SAN FRANCISCO

Cambridge, Hagerstown, New York, Philadelphia, Washington
London, Mexico City, São Paulo, Singapore, Sydney

Portions of this book first appeared in *Christian Century* and *Currents in Theology and Mission*.

A MINIATURE CATHEDRAL AND OTHER POEMS. Copyright © 1987 by Walter Wangerin, Jr. All rights reserved. Printed in the United States of America. No part of this book may be used or reproduced in any manner whatsoever without written permission except in the case of brief quotations embodied in critical articles and reviews. For information address Harper & Row, Publishers, Inc., 10 East 53rd Street, New York, N.Y. 10022. Published simultaneously in Canada by Fitzhenry & Whiteside Limited, Toronto.

FIRST EDITION

Designed by Donald Hatch

Library of Congress Cataloging-in-Publication Data

Wangerin, Walter.
    A miniature cathedral and other poems.

    I. Title.
PS3573.A477M5 1987   811'.54   86–45831
ISBN 0-06-069257-X
ISBN 0-06-069264-2 (paperback)

87 88 89 90 91 HC 10 9 8 7 6 5 4 3 2 1

This, with all my heart, for Thanne

CONTENTS

ix

PREFACE

While I prepared this book for publication, there was a long period when I considered calling it *Three Cycles: Exercises in Poetry.* The first element in such a title was impersonal and reasonable enough. I meant by it to indicate a certain self-conscious parallelism, both thematic and artistic, among the cycles that compose the greatest portion of the book, so that each might be seen to illuminate, somewhat, the other two.

But the second element of that title was probably too personal altogether, because it was too self-conscious. I'm aware of the difference between practicing, and practicing *at,* poetry. Both know poetic form very well; but while the first obeys form into invisibility (observing the laws of literary convention so well that the good poem appears to have satisfied nothing but its own existence), the second but strives to obey—so that both the striving and the form are left apparent in the end, more or less friends with one another. I think that I've made friends with poetry and its form. But I fear that most often I do only just make friends with it. "Exercises" are the pupil's way of practicing at poetry. I wanted "Exercises" in the title so no one would suppose that I had fooled myself regarding the achievement of this material. I was saying, "Please don't mind if I love the form in public, more often dancing with her than dying into her. It's a chance to show her off, after all. And seeing that we both know the true nature of the book, accept it for what it is: Exercises in poetry."

Too personal. And likely too oblique as well. So the title was changed and the little apologia tucked into a preface.

But a preface is a serviceable alternative after all, because it gives me the opportunity to say one or two things clearly about the parts of the book and something about their dance with form.

Cycle One

This is a narrative, a story. It would be a mistake, then, to assume that the speaker is the author. Rather, he's a character of the piece—though he is also, in this fiction, a poet.

The fact that he speaks in sonnets is no accident to his personality, his condition, his development, or to my composition. This is how poetic form and character combine: at first the narrator chooses the sonnet as a challenge by which to impress the woman he loves—a little like Tom Sawyer's walking the picket fence for the heart of Becky Thatcher. But then, when he must speak a grief too great for him, he absolutely needs the control, the cold restraint of the sonnet's fixed form. The sonnet form becomes itself a quality of acting—not unlike his wife's gestures of denial in the face of death. She pulls weeds and falls into a stony silence. But he is a poet, incapable of silences; therefore, though he sublimates his feeling in metaphor (form is a quality of character), he talks, he talks and exasperates her by his talking. But form may manifest the tension within him as well as that between them; for even the indifferent sonnet fails him. "Ashes, Ashes," a sort of mad effusion about madness, lacks a fourteenth line and should, to the unconscious expectations in the reader's ear, feel vaguely unfinished, indeterminate, unfulfilled.

This is a single example of the use of form.

And I imagine the whole cycle to be like skimming a stone thirty-three times across the face of a smooth water: each poem is a splash; and though much of the experience of these two characters is skipped over, yet the individual poems send out concentric circles of meaning and implications which finally overlap—if the reader is patient and willing to follow the radiations—until the characters' entire history is by indirections accounted for.

Cycle Two

These poems are joined like those in Cycle One, the skimming of the stone. But these are personal, as the title declares, "My People."

They are arranged in a generally chronological order, the first ones being written twenty years ago, the last only recently, and those between, occasionally—as there was an event or a feeling that wanted memorialization, communication, or understanding. Essentially, then, most of them have served very practical purposes within the context of my life, actually participating in the experiences they refer to.

Cycle Three

If Cycle One describes the evolution of two characters and their relationship, Cycle Three presents the evolution of a theme, a repeated *anagnorisis,* again and again the recognition of human finitude which is received differently at the different stages of one's life.

The Christ Mass

I consider this to be a single poem consisting of five parts and a thematic rehearsal called a Reprise. Certainly, no part could stand on its own; and no strophe or its antistrophe is complete until one has illuminated both. As the Greek tragedian chorus walked to the right, it sang the strophe; it was not done until, singing the antistrophe, it walked back to the place whence it began. Or perhaps it danced both fro and to. In either case, its steps were measured, and each motion had its obverse. So here.

Prologue: The Light-Man's Apology

I could impale his face, sir,
In solid, eternal lights,
Or bleach it and leech it of grace, sir,
By stroboscopic bites;

But if it's all the same to you,
I'd just as soon
A sudden, occasional, sulphurous match
In Darby's condemned saloon.

A
MINIATURE
CATHEDRAL
AND OTHER POEMS

.

CYCLE ONE:

Intimacy
(A Narrative)

A Miniature Cathedral

I hold a miniature cathedral just
Before me; I lift it in a hush of silent
Whispers and hold it here above the dust;
And just before my face I lift an island.

And I must call it "island" since it holds
No conversation with reality—
Save that I have thought of it. Yet it folds
A beauty in its being that is me:

For it shall be—and say it: It shall be!
For I shall step a moment up to you
And tender you a wrapped reality;
I'll walk from shades and speak from purple blends:

"While everyone was busy making friends
With you . . . I fell in love with you.
I fell in love with you."

If Not Juan, a John May Recommend Me

I'm twenty-two and thick—thick fingered; thick,
Gross, halt in my walking; thick in the moods
That muddy me; helpless to turn a quick
Grin to someone's wit; hanging with the foods
I do not taste while I still chew on them;
Ponderous, a mountain trying to see
The sun, then waiting till it come to him;
I've little eyes and lenses thick as trees.

Oh, but I have a voice like chrism, I!
I'm Chrysostom, forever fervid; I,
The Baptist, strike the dry blue dome of sky
To ringing with my clapper tongue, and high
On Patmos sing a sword between my teeth.
How lithe's my love!—if you won't look but listen when I speak.

But Speak the Word Only

Things happen in the naming. "Light!" said God;
At once light straked the nothingness—from no
Where, from the mouth of God. No, it was not
As though bright, fiery horses reared, as though
They plunged mane-flaming through the dark because
God ordered them abroad, lights lighting out
At God's command. The speaking didn't cause
Light. His word *was* light, primal in his mouth.

Naming things creates them. Look out! I stand
At the black rim of the universe, on nothing,
Facing you, about to talk. Not command—
I won't command nor ask nor risk rebuffing.

No, I will merely say the word, and we
Will be, and you will be in love with me.

The Burning Ones

—But when we came to it, what did I say?
Holy God, the room was full of smoke,
Stinging my eyes, shrouding the barkeep so
Dismally that he seemed ascending o-
Ver glowing roach clips, grinning at the joke;
A waitress next arose through murk to lay
Our table with two discs for drinks; a grey
Old man threw back his head and laughed. You spoke.
I sat staring: How could these three just blow
About the room, a 'keep, a man so old
His eyes were ash, a waitress rushing cokes?
Wings! Each, six finny wings! I froze, afraid.
  In the day when, mute, I thought that I would die,
   You touched my lips with coals. You spoke—not I.

The Ascension

Ha! With little contemplation, without
The estimate of public standards, I
Have found this body wanting nothing by
Another nothing, and I can speak about
Perfection where it blunders, for throughout
Its imperfection it is loved. Then cry,
Shout, bellow like the bull, my body, my
Enormous corpse—and if you can, then flout
Your dress of death and, heaven help you, dance!
With no thought at all I exult in the mere
Suspiration of my soul. Advance
The spheres, my soul. I've found you worthy: where
Another sees your worth, dearly she proves it,
Proving her own—and, soul, thou art beloved!

Reversals on the Fall

I fell, Lord God, in love—and then ensued
No less than the Genesitic wonder: I
Discovered a land, a primal continent
Within me; I roared, I gorged its orchards, spent
My breath to gather pleasant fruits and try
Those less than pleasant. All this coast was new
And I climbed high, observing a lunging view.
When next I found that I was loved, that my
America was claimed, possession went
To her, and *then* I turned obedient:
I, sinless, civilized, devout, the shy
First man in Eden, the very image of you!
   Would it trouble you, at your return, to see
   Yourself the snake, and she Divinity?

The Better Question

So who made who love who? Forget almighty
God, who maketh weal and woe together
Indiscriminately, just as flighty
As a pigeon dropping slops wherever
Wind and whim decide. He's arbitrary,
After all, his "weal and woe" a dreary
Exercise to prove on us (to practice
For his own assurances) his mono-
Most-supernal-all-sufficient-cactus-
Lonely Godness. "I AM": *I go solo.*

So who made who love who? You, me? Or was it
I caused love in you?
                      But she with cusséd
Pedantry replies: "Not who, but whom.
I love just one: the boy whom God consumes."

Just Ironies, My Love

If you have cause to accuse me of taints
Or sorceries or some insinuating
Magic, and if the proof of these complaints
Demands my punishment, then I am waiting.
I confess my craft. But hear first what fraction
Of me deserves disgrace; to the rest be kind.
My legs you may not scourge for subtle action;
They never sinewed through the night to find
The dry lynx of En-dor nor knelt to her.
My lips, for all their black conjunctions, knew
No words but those young mothers learn to purr.
But my poems wove your two eyes closed, so
Sinking you in the same dark that darkened me.
I gave you you, the potion—now the penalty.

The Necklace

Thomas! Thomas, no! Are you reading these
Sonnetized knots for their involving threads,
Their riddled inconsistencies? Then please—
Return them and yourself depart. They're beads.
They bead. They're written to bead, like spiders' webs
That string in dawn a thousand dew drops, one
Of which can dart your sight and drop you dead
With the purest ray of amber of the sun.
They're beads, refracting laughter. I want to stun
You with one color from the spectrum of
Her laughter. Thomas! Her radiant joy is sun-
Light. My prisms darken, parted from her love.
　　Clasp them, the subtle weave and beads and all,
　　Above her breast, and watch the world burn beautiful.

On Memory

So one moment has become a nut
Of everlasting sweetness and of
Everlasting closure, both; the meat, shut
In an immortal shell, is tucked above
The shouting mortality of my tasting tongue.
(A necessary contrast: things sublime,
The deathless things, are manifest among
Things mouldering; eternity needs time.
The indivisible is proved by parts,
While time is measured in eternity—
But neither meets except in the transfixer, Me!)
Lo: I have forever what Forever has held
Back from me . . .
                    I spoke with my love; two hearts
Divided into one; a certain meld
Developed in this single memory:
We spoke and, speaking, touched eternity.

Gentle Rejection

This woman tells me "No" as small as grass:
      "No" as if it was
    A SHELL sign turning down
And distant in a morning mountain town.

Gentle Consent

"Hey!" he cried.
She looked around.
He kissed her sound
Upon the
        "Hey!"
She cried. "If you
Were not—"
           She lied;
And tell me, who
Can blame their
         "Hey,"
Tiptoeing away?

BoysWish

I watched the boy wish to smile
And almost want to laugh.
Instead he sat awhile,
His poor head bent by half
And half to the plain table
Before him—a boy unable.

Yesterday I didn't laugh.
You did. Because of me.
And then by half and half
I fell to grinning because we
Are first of all a joke and after
That a brilliant fit of laughter.

Coming (i)

When you come to me biting your lip
Like linen and remorse, when you
Stand in my door, stand in my room
And call me with your eyes to help
You with the thing that brought you here
But fled you at the coming, when
You are a white Christ-candle here,
Silent, robed and pale and still
And waiting—what will I say to you?

Epithalamium

My silent bride! Once in a lifetime
The cicada rises and splits her back;
She cracks the calcified husk of an old age
The way we pop a peanut open.

Once in a lifetime she labors wavingly
Outside herself—her natal, pale-green,
Crumpled wings unwrinkling to the weather:
She leaves her shell, her image, and she flies.

But a boy once touched the wing of a hatching cicada—
And it bled, in cellophane, with a terrible ease,
One green drop:
An emerald hung in a thin wing sac.

The boy tingled, so pure, so deep,
So lovely was that drop. But this was lifesblood,
And the same boy grieved for what he'd done.
    The boy was me.

My silent bride—so am I now
The old cicada young again.
Elizabeth, I've split an envelope
Of poses, certitudes, and hard age.

I've labored, loving you, outside myself,
Escaped my likeness, this calcified visage,
Am unwrinkling in a chill wind to fly.
    And lo, I bleed.

Coming (ii)

Suddenly winter will have at you all
In the swoop of a small
Snowflake –
And more than whole fields of white snow,
More than the months when you cannot know
For Christ's sake
When another human being will break
Through the snow to your home,
You will be afraid.
And then I will come.

Coming (iii)

In the most tender silence have I come
To look at you. There is no coming more
Soft than that I've waked up. I'm home. I'm home.
It is from a long dream that I've returned
In which dream, dear, I saw that you were dead.
No fright was in this thing and, strangely, no
Thought you'd gone away. In my dream I said,
"I'm sad, Elizabeth," and no one swore
Me deeper sorrow; no one could, although
They might have wondered why I didn't weep.
That wasn't in me, dear. You are asleep.
You are asleep. Your face is just the same
As in my dream; and though I wasn't turned
To tears in dreaming, that I'm crying now is not my shame.
I'm home. I'm home, Elizabeth. Shh, do you hear the rain?

Coming (iv)

One stump twice my size,
The stem of a storm-tormented sycamore,
Sheared, splintered at a violent angle,
Stripped to the heartwood, pith, the open core—

One old trunk has thrown back its head
In gaunt supplication; all
Its gut is caught in a tight twist
Of fiber: pain is general—

But
I will find you home tonight
And
It will die.

Coming (v)

I know the pressure of her breathing. I feel
In darkness now its rise and fall beside
My arm: A moment up a moment deals
Me a small consent, rises to confide
Her spirit to me in a touch of truth;
A moment down a moment closes the touch
With a religious finishing (this much
I know without a word spoken to soothe
Or startle the time into reality)
—Closes, because another takes its rise
From there, its soft assent from there, from me
And from my sleeper's breathing. She breathes, she lies
Against the tender of my arm, and I,
I rage that one time she will close and die!

Closure

Between two fingers her nipple appears
A soft, searching tongue,
Two dots of milk printed at the tip of it;
Her full hand cups the breast.

How obedient is her breast,
Spilling through her hand!

She's tipped her head sideways,
Gazing blamelessly at the intimacy
Exposed, her hair spilling all on the left side
Like black water breaking at her ear,
Pouring on the forehead of the baby,
Babe, baby, in the crook of her arm.

How full her face is of that child,
And full her flesh is for him.

I think her lips are fuller now, too,
Rolling outward like a pout.
She breathes deeper, the air more rich to her,
Sparkling with gladness, her nostrils distended:
These are as mature as my mother's, once.

This baby curves his tongue, when he cries,
Like a spoon, the rim quivering.
I think it must be a strong muscle,
Not gentle—utilitarian
On this most private, yielding flesh of my wife
Which has neither muscle nor bone
To stand up for itself.

Little truckdriver! That is no
Dashboard knob to yank at!

But she cuts pigeon sounds in her throat,
And the infant leans,
And her nipple fits into his mouth,
And he smacks, his eyes closed,
Sighing between swallows;
And so does she—sigh.

While I feel alien. Never
Did she spill so willingly for me.

Please, Come –

If the sunset is a brass tension
When the day and the dusk like angry stags
Clash antlers in the clouds,
Then what is the night but their enwreathing
After all –
    When each one bleeds
    Into the other, whose bloods
    Are peace and prayer and natural?

This, diurnal, is the evening:
Anger lags;
The darkness swells in universal breathing;
All the small deer lay them down in leaves;
And we may go to bed –

Oh, please! I pray the natural,
Enweaving, sweet, conciliating night upon our tension
After all –
    If all of these,
    Then why not we?
    Please, come to bed with me.

Stealing Away

Now you know all the sounds.
Dogs moan —
The dogs of the darkness moan
Like engines agonizing against
Too huge a load,
Trucks in low gear
Trying and trying, winding the slow shaft up the hill.

You know the night sounds.
Cats cry —
The gaunt cats cry
Like children in shocked sorrow
Hugging the posts of wooden porches
And sliding to the floor in helpless slowth,
Abandoned.

You know the sounds.
Motherhood has given you ears.
Solitude gives me mine.
Motherhood nightly
Steals my wife away from me
To see if the sounds are her son.

Parting (i)

I walked back to the schoolyard. When I came
I took her hand. They hadn't said the boy
Had died decapitated, head and frame;
They'd only told me (eyes on my chin, coy
As girls or criminals) the boy was dead.
I'd gone down to the tracks to see; and now,
Strong, strong, Elizabeth, be strong, I said
The same—how that the boy was dead, but not how.

"Come home," I said.
                   "Wait," she said, "wait."
                                  I felt
Her thumb forcing her hand from mine. She knelt
Down by the sidewalk.
                 "Wait."
                        And she pulled weeds.
Her skirt strained higher than the shave-line. Weeds!—
Black fingers furious in the dirt: "They ought
To be ashamed. This isn't neat. It's *not!*"

Parting (ii)

But the leaves of the green tree
Are the soil that feeds
Leaves on a green tree, dear!

Come, climb Olympus: look down and see
Time inside itself, and flowers inside their seeds;
One tree's a forest, one wood a hemisphere.

Say that our son was the leaf
That curled like a hand in prayer and intercedes
(Sweet sacrifice) in all the children here—

No? A stupid conceit? Then you be
Leaves and I, my soul, the soil: fall down. Concede
Yourself and all your grieving to my care.

Oh please be one with me!
If all of these, then why not we?
Elizabeth please come to bed with me.

Parting (iii)

She says I talk like the jay,
Like a preacher untouched by the grief he presumes
    to explicate,
Like a poet.

She says this with her ineffable eyes,
In furious silence, standing at the stove,
Her teardrops spitting one by one in the hot grease—oh!

She says this by her untouchable posture,
In meals too much for two of us to eat—
Uttering not a word of it herself.

So what should I do?
Fall silent too?
And be eaten up with what I do not say?

Parting (iv)

The steel needle floats on the surface
Of a water tight unto itself.
This phenomenon is called cohesion,
The repelling property of liquids still,
Still undisturbed, still wilfully indifferent —

You, my wife:
To touch with my threaded fingertip
Your lips
And so to sew them one with peace;
To trace the trail of tears
That runs thin, linear
From your eye, the dayspring,
To the evening fountain of your throat;
And next to rest upon your skin
(Water-skin, beaded into being
Because there is a dreadful stillness
Underneath the surface;
Water-skin, because it films
On your internal, terse restraint,
And I'd float lightly on that film);
To know you by a motion not
Your own but mine
                    — Christ! that would shame me should
You move to answer and I
Had nothing left but guilt. Why,
I should sink like a shivered
Needle and drown — but not in you.

I'd drown in the abysmal need that made me
Move at all. So let it go.
I hold still, and I touch nothing.
So let it be.
You sit on your side of the bed,
I lie on mine,
Fingers pencil-dry at prayer:
Just so. And so.

Parting (v)

Talk to me! Talk! My love affair is with
The night: its heart's the darknesses. I am
As near as far from it, may as well damn
Its black rotundity as damn a myth
And either way be my own audience
And my own mark since either way the night
Abides and holds my soul within its dense
Nothingness—where this soul revolves and might
Return upon itself, with pity, pride
(If circling back achieved companionship)
But can't so much as . . . *My son has died!*
Jesus, the thought drives me straight—like a whip.
    I found my wife mute, entoiled in fright: fright.
    I stood beside her bed. Inside the night.

Ashes, Ashes

Listen! When Mike my brother made a fire
Of bedsheets in our room with matches he
Was not supposed to have, I knocked him down;
I broke his nose; and while he scrambled round
My back like a fat spider, my one free
Hand beat the flames and we became a choir
Of little curses one against the other,
And when the sheets were black I had become
His savior. I saved him. Since then he's slept in some
Clinic and eaten clinic food but Father
Said he's as well as can be expected what
With the circumstances which are that he's not
Well at all but insane and he's my brother—

Nightcrawlers

Where have I seen this mass before,
Years, years ago? —
Why, fishing: a boy rowed out from shore
With a thin cane pole,

A tin can and damn little skill.
Trying to turn
He slued the boat — and the can spilled
Out a fist of worms,

Bait! Just such a lump is on
The table here
Between us, like dinner undone.
It's your heart, my dear.

Dark Prisms,
Sonnets Without Sunlight

Am I glass? Has the thick boy gone thin glass?
Well, sometimes I despair because I was
Not seen—beheld. Beheld's a better word.
I want gripping with her eyes; to be searched;
To have the obscure runes of me sought—held.
Held is the better word. For years I'd spelled
Alone each letter of my flesh, rehearsed
Compulsively my private alphabet;
For years this cheap grammatic would have bored
Me or belittled me or, better, would
Have mortified me outright, but for this:
For years it was a warrant of the good
To come, when she would see—behold. Hold—possess.
Dear God, the worst word is Inadequate!

Parting (vi)

The lid sprang open on its own— No, no;
No, that's a lie. I hadn't seen the brooch
She kept closed in her jewelry box for so
Long, it seemed a dear thing lost. I approached,
Unlocked the lid, and, on the formal blood-snow
Of velvet, found her cameo.

Dirt, like fingernail dirt,
Was worked
Into the corner of its eye;
The chin was precious with a high,
Tiny nick;
The hair, the carven hair—the hair was dun;
And the cheek had been riddled by some quintessential
     pick,
Like freckles gone to tears, gone to the crow—
Gone:
My gift, our marriage, and her cameo.

But how could I request divorce? That too,
Too much requires a faith in something new.

Departure –

H ow can I leave you? How can I walk away?
E ncourage me. I walk on trust, and even
A t death, especially at death, I may
V enture nothing unless commanded, driven.
E very memory that you have given
N ature's slower learner, every word

S aid, was a little life which now must heaven
P ut to death in me with an accurate sword.
O r else let the electric cords that poured
K inetic life between us twist and break.
E ncourage me – please! Speak to me what toward

Y ou heaven spoke: heaven said that you could speak.
O n your *Fiat* I came, a flaming horse;
U tter *Anathema* and we'll divorce.

Sutter's Fence at Dusk

The fence is a black sentence on the snow;
Walk on, walk on.
As long as you walk on
It tells you with its imprint what you know,
That the sky's not black alone, but has spun
Night throughout the earth and will
Weave this *Dēmen* till it's done:
Until the birds, and the unhappy mice, and you, my son,
Are still.

CYCLE TWO:

My People

Courting You, My Diminution

Twice, Thanne, have I been with you long enough
    To leave you with a kiss;
Each time I thought I'd plumbed the reasons why
    You smile and what your silence is,
But these must be as visceral and new
    As every minute is—
Because what might have turned to take my hand
    Could turn away my kiss.

Should I revise my reckoning and think,
    Instead of kissing you,
A minute well indented with my love,
    The mere minute will do?

Tomorrow, Thanne, I'll visit you like this:
    For a minute . . . for a kiss.

Courting You, the Private You

Yours is a museum effort at talk.
Between one word and another I've
An even mile and silence for the walk;
Between this gallery and the next I move
In short, reporting periods
Of step and stepping,
Half expecting
The custodial God
To be sweeping in your marble corridors and quietude,
His broom collecting
What it was you did not
Say.
Yet always, Louvre, when I gaze
At you,
My thought
Is this: *How Silence becomes you!*

Courting You, the Lowly You

R est easy, girl: your five-foot-three
U pstanding posture could not be
T oo poor, too down-pretending, where
H eaven himself is moved to care
A bout the toss you give your hair.
N ever think it easier
N or accidental that he bends
E nough to come confuse the ends

(B right ends, the blowing, tendril ends)
O f your loose hair. Rather, Thanne, think
H ow many light-years he must shrink
L ittler to reach the little you.
M uch good it will do him, though. *I* can do
A s well for strictures, and for skill—the same!
N ot with my diminishing, but with your name.

Engagement

As sadness has it, this ring will have to be mine.
What's everlasting in its round concern
In me is linear: I will forget
I love you. Mind you, not stop loving, yet
Stop remembering. Then let me return
To the peak diamond, to the ascendant sign
Of a love that never left. The ring is mine.

But as happiness will have it, it is your
Ring, Thanne, your finger and your self. It's you
Who bears extraneous what's given for
Utility to me; I have to heed
What you have but to wear. Ruthanne, you *are*,
And you're the radius of my love: You need
No ring to be nor to be loved; I do,
To seize love and to be. The ring is you.

> *Great God, in whom we trust!—*
> *But make us something*
> *Greater than this ring:*
> *Make us the circle, and encircle us.*

Second Thoughts

i.

As I understand it, a triumph's a wedding,
A charge to the rail, a retreat to the bedding—
But who will enlighten my father's first son
And tell me with sympathy which of us won?

ii.

Or think of engagement as weary surrender,
The end of a prancing, magnificent bender:
I watch what Finalities limit my sin,
And fear for the Hang-over soon to set in.

iii.

Merciful God, won't you countenance wending?
Must all of your pathways be straight and unbending?
A mouth to the south of me which was my mother,
While forth to the north of me, lo! is another—
But God saith: *Through much tribulation and sorrow
Ye enter the Kingdom.* I marry tomorrow.

Circus

I march to trumpets and endorse the idiot
Confusion of snare drums when I perform;
Trombones are the tide behind, and women giddy at
The slashed red of my howling uniform.

I ride elephants, scorn lions, embrace
Giraffes; I trust that Heaven is no higher
Than a particular, pluperfect wire;
And when I breathe, enormous tents take place.

The towns I enter shake sleep from their eyes,
Stand up, and wonder if they shouldn't cheer;
The children do; then stores go blank and here
And there a man starts grinning past surprise.

The calico towns say Yes: a stripèd, violent parade
They, Yes! have room for. Thanne, you are the village I
    invade.

The Covenant:
Καὶ ἐσκήνωσεν ἐν ἡμῖν

The tent took wind in deep
Redundant swallows,
Bent low and rolled to keep
Its several hollows

Dry, then rose again.
Here was no pride:
The simple complement
Of one inside.

—The wedding day,
August 24, 1968

Grace: The Veiled (the Veil) Revealed

Comes the morning, and dim
Unwitnessed spider webs
Shine, tiny chandeliers;
The spider strings small crystal on a whim,
In her warrings engineers
A truce, this delicate gauze her diagram
(*Here I am!*)
This melting gauze a revelation
Outfacing fears—
Darkness ebbs;
The dawn is washed in consecration;
And dew on my garden
Grants her hidden habitation
Pardon.

Comes mourning, and my silent wife
Lifts up her eyes: the webs around
Them have gone damp with sorrow, strife,
A sudden revelation, care.
Lo! All the walk-ways of her soul are wound
Up wet and visible and there.

Dear Thanne:

This poem is to woo you
To the close consideration of two
Eggs:

Marry one—with Oscar Mayer
Sausages—to butter in a frier,
This for dinner;

Allow the other one the leisure
To con-descend to the ascending pleasure
Of a sinner;

Your husband begs
Two eggs
For dinner and for ardor,
Not in that order.

Skip Winter!

There *is*, after all, Thanne;
But Thanne is, all of a sudden,
Drowsy,
And then she is asleep—
And all because I had an expectation
(I had not single)
Thwarted,
I am lonelier tonight than the solitary tree
Whose shivering leaves were, all of them, dead but could
Not fall.

I am the urge toward summer
In autumn.

Annunciation

```
. . ... . .TH ✠ . . . . . . . ✠ . . . . E
. E AR. . .T . ✠ . . . . . . . ✠ .H. . . .
. . A. . . ... ✠ . . . .N. . ✠ . . .D.
. . ... . .T. ✠ H . .ANN . ✠ . . . . E
. . ... ... ✠ . . .A . N . ✠ . . .D.
. . ... ... ✠ . . . . . . . ✠ . .I. . .
WE ARE WITH ✠ . . . . . . . ✠ CHILDE
            ✠ HOSANNA ✠
```

—Christmas Greeting, 1969

Anniversary

i.

T hou art my wife as thou
H ast been my wife for six
A ltricial years, but now—
N ow comes the crucifix;
N ow come the crossing sticks:
E ach year shall twist and meet itself upon thy brow . . .

ii.

But   I
Re   l y
Upon   that   crucifixion   there
That wrinkled consequence of care
For   it
I s   m e
Well knit
In   thee

My Children—The Shorter Cycle

i.

T ell me, girl: How is it you can rust
A t three? The talk scrapes in your throat
L ike hinges like to bust;
I dle joints lock and loose on a corrosive note;
T iny flecks of oxide make your glances bold—
H ow is it, girl, that rust on you is just
A nother brown more beautiful than gold?

ii.

J ack Ketch, my sons have seen you!
O n a tight October morning have
S een you gibbet a million rattled leaves —
E ach leaf a sinew
P opped, each fall a potter's field and grave —
H ave seen you, Jack, and laughed at you!

iii.

M y sons heard rhythm in the falling leaves.
A   rhythm's always an occasion for
T he dance, so they danced! They danced like the poor;
T hey thumped it like berries in a metal pot,
H arrowed together a mountain of compost gore,
E xcited the wind to a deeper declarative roar,
W ent down with a laugh they had not laughed before—

iv.

M ake three angels in the snow,
A geless, cold, and hollow;
R emind me once before you go
Y ou, too, were here—then follow.

Whence This Tree of Knowledge

We'd been walking the countryside an hour
When Mary slipped my hand and dashed ahead.
You! Barefoot girl, don't climb crab apple trees.
The tree crouched like a cripple, one arm sore,
Held akimbo, while others dangling dead.
Mary, don't— A crab tree shorter than me,
An old man leering, a diminutive,
Diseased old man. *Don't!* It seemed to have lost
An eyeball to the digging squirrel, and like
A blind socket this frowning knothole writhed
Tendons inside itself, staring. "Come, give
Me your flesh, girl," it breathed, and Mary crossed
Its cankered branch with her white leg. "I'll spike
You, girl," it whispered. Suddenly it scythed
A narrow limb in Mary's loin where she
Sat straddle at the trunk. *God damn it!* Had
The child forgot? I taught her! *Mary, see
Evil everywhere!* I taught her, taught her. . . .

O Fathers, good, strong, honest, brave—and mad,
Loving dements us, and menaces our daughters.

Kinder- und Hausmärchen

i.

My mother's tongue was wooden, straight, a broom
Projecting from her mouth, her hair the brambles.
She cleaned house like the north wind, cold, white, grim —
Jakob! Wilhelm! You found her *ungesammelt*
In god knows what thatched *Bauern* cottages:
What did it serve, putting her back together?
Philology? *Recchelees* sciences!
My mother's tongue was wooden. Write that, after
You've written how she licked my skin the way
The medieval bear licked cubs to shape.
My mother's mouth was wooden. Dodgson may
Have met her peppered — yes: but he escaped
To *clepe* her "Duchess." I (my mother's face
Was Teuton) lived the tale as commonplace. . . .

ii.

Blame, so we blame her—but who thinks the tale
Which tells his childhood governed, too, his mother?
What could she choose to do? If she were frail
The work would kill her: *storm, then, through another
Summer.* If she were passionate, they'd damn
Her for a gypsy; passion, though, was proper
For rearing proper, upright children: *one
Became the other.* If she wept at color,
Words, dusk, the lark, or thought, they'd cluck and sing
Of Bedlam; if she laughed too longingly
Or loose, her uterus was wandering—
So rage found reason in her progeny.
    Peter, Peter! You made that woman wild
    You kept inside the pumpkin of your child.

iii.

I remember your cellar, now. Do you?—
Clean concrete tubs, a glass-ribbed scrubbing board,
And a smell—(Grandma had dry buttocks, bald
Armpits, leather intestines, a mouth that chewed
Blasphemies silently, although the Lord
God still issued commandments she still heard,
Adding them chunk by chunk to the coal pile,
Stirring a Sinaitic dust)—the smell
Grandma had was the odor in your cel-
Lar, remember? It was the house you grew
Up in. Here is my question: had you, too,
For lies, to bite Fels Naphtha soap—and chew?
       Mother, Mother, Gretel! We had one mother
       After all! I'm Hänsel. I am your brother.

iv.

Yes, there were giants in those days and in
Our world. Yes, they despised you. And yes, they'd
Kill you if they could. But you couldn't slay
Them—so it was a standoff, stick for sin.

Giants: Sweet Acid Gossip, gross as air—
You smelled your name in the breeze like wet hair;
Outdoors you grew fearful, but indoors you
Grew furious, fumbling for what to do.

Giants: those women all were members of
One body, like a ball of bees, a fist
Of snakes, or Jesus. To assault or love
Them singly killed no more than cut a mist.

Giants! So you sent me forth, full of rage—
Your rage, though it felt like mine; full of rage—
For them, though it felt like me; full of rage,
Like a knot stick thrust in my throat, a rage

To beat your giants with: *Stick, beat! Stick, beat!*
The stick said, *Whom?* But I, a child, said, "Me."

v.

Mother Holle, do you know how much I loved you?
Under the well and in its meadows—do you know?
It was I who shook down red ripe apples when they
    begged me,
I who shook your feather ticking, making snow.

Under the well, in sunken meadows, in the cottage
Where you dwelt dreamly, Mother, I obeyed you well.
In the glare light of common day we were another
Pair, *hässliches*, perhaps—but my yearning cast such spells!

I rose from the well wet with gold (all this is true)
And I, flushed with obedience and its reward,
Came home: *Unser goldener Junge is wieder hie!*
You rushed to me, you lady longing rich young lords. . . .

Never (I breathed submerged, I breathed through large
    eyes, through
Wish within that well) *never* did I not love you!

vi

And now I search the bloodred rose
Whose center cups one pearl (a dew
Drop, beautiful and trembling) whose
Charm is the *Schamir,* to undo

The doors, to set the captives free.
I dreamed you were a nightingale.
Zicküt was all you croaked for me.
A wire cage kept you, and travail —

I dreamed the bloodred rose, its touch
Alone, would spring that cage and hush
Your grief and shift your shape, all three.

The bloodred rose, too, grows encaged.
Bones are its bars — but I will break
My breast to break you, Mother, free.

Father, Look At Me Looking At You

W hen have we seen our changing in a glass?
A rrest me in your mirror and I will
L oose my habilimental privacy
T ruly to smile at you; smile back at me.
E ncounter my laughter; laugh back—remarkable!
R emark it: me, you, is, to be, and was!

W hen has anyone seen new wrinkles screw
A round his face, or watched age grace him, till
N ow? And mere reflected smiles are spectral, thin;
G lassy smiles fade as soon as guilt or sin
E rase the smile progenitor. But *my* guilt,
R eflected in *my* progenitor—in you—
I s atoned, and lo! One smile remains.
N o, two; but two's one in the glass of our singular names.

For My Solitary Brother:
Kohoutek, Come!

P art of me knows a part of you,
H ails you at a distance, and waits.
I watch your streaking through the night:
L iquid remorse and fire, that sight
I s comet's breath and supplicates.
P oach the night, dear brother; scarf it; hack and spew

W eird silence. I watch. And I will wait for you.

—In the same month and year
that the comet Kohoutek appeared

Lines for a Reliquary Bone

C ut on the angle of a buzzard's wing,
I nclining toward some convalescent plane,
N ow see this piece, this wedge, this Cindy-thing,
D ug from her leg to ease her leg of pain,
Y et saved to souvenir the suffering—
'S *wounds!* the girl wastes nothing, neither bone nor bane.

Keepsake

Oh, my children! What can I bequeath
You more than stories? Lips don't last: they dry
Soon, tremble soon, and die; but that they breathed
Warm words against your flesh and kissed your eyes—
That will remain in memory a story.
All of the goods I leave you you will use
Up, digging out the goodness as they quarry
Carrara: I can't stay in what you choose
To change—and you *will* choose when I cannot.
But stories deep as fairy tales, as searching
As poetry, as hoary, unforgot
And vulvar as the *Heilsgeschichte,* cursing
And blessing at once—these stand mining (whether
I'm dead, ye delvers, or alive) forever.

CYCLE THREE:

The Young, the Old—and Aging (The Seasons)

Parturition: Her Confusion

I thought he said, "Appease the God in me,"
    And laughed.
He hadn't: inappropriate response.
It's time, his eyes said, *for solemnity;*
    His craft
Consumed him as a flame sucks wax and sconce—

I swear he said, "Appease the God in me"!
    I screamed,
Leaning gut-forward, legs and mouth apart,
Pushing the lump of holy hurt which he,
    I dreamed,
Demanded out my body: "Here! My heart!"

Jesus! The man (*appease the God in me*)
    He laid
The numb edge of the knife to my extreme
Self, my deepest womanhood, and he,
    He made
A cut; at once blood rushed in a red stream

Down my buttocks—*Please the God in me!*
    And white
As wax was my split skin, and drained dead grey,
While he was bowed, masked and frowning furiously. . . .
    O bright
Good God, why must the baby come this way?

Contractions

The ukase of a red, elliptic scream—
    A doctor hears and doubts it.

The forehead mortified in worming pain—
    A nurse regards and daubs it.

The belly elemental in its crush—
    A mother leans and shouts it.

The moment starving toward its end: the rush—
    A baby sucks air, bucks, and bawls it.

And while the infant, life-struck, lies beside
A hissing tube which issues oxygen
Like a fang, pinking his nose, flesh and feet,
His mother has not yet laid her work aside—
Groans, breathes and sweats; leans, breathes and bears again,
An afterbirth, the heart which does not beat.

Time in a Little:

After Birth

They bathed the bloodshot
Babe, washed scarlet to white snow:
Cold, mortal baptism.

Vent

Time is the nostril
In the baby's face: pink, now
It will blow up black.

Clockwork

The big hand is the
Come-again hand; the little
One is forever.

Issue

I wonder how much
Death throes are like giving birth
To death. I will know.

Initiation: Five Years Old

Timothy, tough as an Old World stoat,
Timothy,
transfixing me
to the side-
walk with his milky American eye—
Timothy made a buzz-saw in his throat;
it cut the curb in two;
it ripped the Avenue
and split
the nodding quietude
of my flannel neighborhood.
Then Timothy spit—
a choked wad
with a pit in the middle
like a rotten apricot,
a huge, a spinning, an enormous load:
Watch out!
His spittle
landed plump between my shoes—*watch out!*
Then his words came floating toward me, fat,
like detonating lozenges:
Don't you step on that—
yes don't; no; don't yes
—or I will kill you, Kraut!

Kill me? Kill me? Knife me in the mouth
so that I'd blubber blood and gout
a puddle in the gutter for the bus
to park in when it did not pick me up?
Kill me? I lifted my hands into the air,
became a root,
and froze beneath his milky stare:
I didn't want to die.

By-and-by
a sweet string pulled in my gut;
it knotted in my bladder—but
I didn't want to die;
taut along my penis—but,
urgent in my under—but,
I had to *go!* I had to, but
I did not want to die!
Timothy! Timothy,
please take away your eye—

"Ow!" I cried,
startling myself, but I
—no good—
I could
not not
cry out—
"OW!"
Oh, *no!* What else could I not not do?
No.
I was too old
for public or for private shamings. No!

I made a resolution, calm and cold:
I spread my arms for balance, raised my shoe,
then stamped it down and squashed his worming spit.

Processional, my arms across my chest
as though I'd taken a penumonic chill,
I walked home. Home, I sent a yellow crest
into the toilet, then turned and sat on it,
and waited for Timothy to come and kill
me there for stepping on his spit.

Initiation: Kleenex, My Wage

I moved down the street in a sort of long stutter.
It was with no sense of importance that
I collected thirty-five cents a house a newspaper;
It was my business, my embarrassing
Business—my fault, then, to stutter. Worse,
It was raining and that made finishing urgent:
My tennis shoes were split rubber.
                                    But Mrs. Dees
Saw me wet and gave me a kleenex to dry
Myself off with and took my time that way
Without really taking my misery.
I left wet, with knots of kleenex on my face
And mulch in my pocket and no thirty-five cents.
I could never collect from her, nor ever
Would. Three days later she opened her neck
Into her bath-tub and all the kleenex in
The city couldn't soak the blood I saw
As all the kleenex in her house had been no
Acceptor of her love—and all the kleenex
In my pocket had dried into a hard little
Ball I could almost *smash her window with!*

Initiation: All the Assaulted

i.

If you were not so frightened, child,
As I am gentle, or
If *I* were crouched—wide-eyed, defiled—
And you the comforter,
Then I would touch you.

But since it is that you are scared
Of me, and since it is
That I have seven years, now, cared
For you, I will not kiss
You, child. Let that be true.

Let that be true along with this,
That when you are asleep
I wonder if an old man's kiss
Would wake you. Oh, I'll keep
That thought a question. Still—
I wonder how to heal this chill.
I wonder what a touch would do
If it were mine to touch you.

ii.

No. Sing another song.
Tell her a certain line
That crouches south along
Her left cheek is a sign.

Tell her you know how old
The grief within her is.
Tell her, "Child, *I* am cold,"
And on that line, a kiss.

Initiation: Litany

A child is dead and seven go to dig
A grave for her. A child is dead and two
Remain behind to watch her bier and by
Their watching are they dead: these two as well
Are dead. (A child was in this city; on
These streets a child was footloose — and I saw her.
I saw these streets with child, and therefore I
May write and say it, and to you and to
This city may I say it: there was a child —
Dear God, there was a child inside this city.)
The seven now have dug their hole outside
The city, so the seven have returned.
They gaze upon the child and watch her bed
And so they too are dead and stand away
From this grey child, and in their standing are they dead.

I met nine children walking, riding out
The city; two sat on a box while seven
Pulled it through the streets and past the gates.
I asked them why they rode and why they walked.
"Because she's dead," these children said to me;
"Because she's dead." I asked them, could I look
And see inside the box and see her dead?
I asked them why they built so large a box
For what must be as minor as a pet.
Nine children heaved and held the lid and stood
Aside that I might see inside this box.
I looked and saw: it might have been a doll,
A dog, a sparrow; looked and saw that it
Was none of those, but a child gone grey; and she was dead.

Nine children go to grave a tenth, and in
Their going carry her grey face inside a box.

I am not going there to bury her
Nor to the hole to see nine cover her.
I am inside this city where a child
Once was, and since I looked upon her bier
And saw her, I am dead and I as well
Most solemnly, most certainly am dead.
I scarcely move; dear God, I scarcely move:
A child is dead, and who that looked on her
Is not? No, none beholding her is not.
A child: *O Kyrie! Eléison!*
Dear God, what will you do with us? A child—
And children bear the body out. *Eléison!*

Youth: How They Do It After All!

Old Corrigen, today, blinked at a jeep
With impudent, screaming sunflowers painted on
Its sides—sides too humble and low to keep

The four sky-laughing youth within; but one
Would grip another at a turn, and so,
Despite the sides, they stayed a group, and none

(Not Corrigen) could blink away the "Oh!
Those Sunflowers!"

Youth: Faith in the In-Finities

Did the moon consider her station too high
To laugh with small children or gladly to shy
    Them a kiss from her lips?
    Poor princess, eclipsed.

When lovers steal forth in the night and in private,
But cover their loving, is she then denied at
    The pleasantest hour?
    Ah, locked in a tower!

    Do fingers patrol her
    To point out her distance?
    Then let me console her
    With gentle insistence:
  The cold and the night and my breath—
  We have brought her to earth in a wreath.

Or: was Luna afraid that her gown was a quality
Women would laugh at?—an ancient banality,
    Linen simplicity,
    White, no variety?

Has she suffered the venom that dribbles from women
Who wear the chameleon and curse the complexion
    That time cannot change?
    In heaven estranged!

    Do fingers patrol her
    To point her apart?
    Oh, let me console her,
    My love and my heart:
I gathered that gown when I caught her
Lovely and laid on the water—

    Celestial light,
    Thou cool, white brow,
    Night's acolyte,
    I have thee now.

Disillusionment:
Summer's End in Storm

Me, closer,
The lightning struts—
On spider's legs comes trembling cross the fields,
The body black above it.

Me, thoughtless,
The lightning thrusts
With heaven-hate the hidden places in the trees
(Oh, *hit* my house! Be done!)

Dumb thunder
Goes slamming into every standing thing
Repeating its impacted promise
Like some irascible gossip of God—Amos!
You! (the discharge)
You're the sinner we mean to stun!

Then, thunder,
Be the tumbling rock your sounding says your are,
Keep the promise,
Crush this skull! Be done!

Come, lightning,
Quit this cracking of your knuckles,
Be the marksman your too-intentional shootings
Boast you to be:
Fire! Fire!
KILL ME—

. . .

Me, deserted:
The fat black spider has passed overhead,
Stuttering stupidly on wilty legs;
She's gone to blushing in the distance.
There's nothing left but a pattering rainfall,
Lies and mild
Piss. Hell—it wa'n't nothin' after all.

Disillusionment:
Time Is a Day and a Night

I find myself regarding the explicit sun
As a reflection:
A pan against the frying atmosphere, a pun,
A tight rejection.

I hate, I hate that hot anathema,
That hounding Gloria—
—until the dusk, the grey
Inglorious eschaton of the day,

When suddenly that firework has become
A moon;
The moon, a numb
Infection,
And the running puss—God help us—gone—
Too soon.

Silent Dialogue

i.

White snow fell in love
With fields of green grass. She said:
Grass, I kiss you gone.

ii.

Branch, I understand
Your lover is the white snow.
Snow, I shake you gone.

iii.

In my windowpanes
Snow whispers: *Wherever I*
Fall, I fall on you.

Schizo

And the Grand Canyon (never seen it)
Ain' no deeper ditch
Than the splayed good-goddam gap
Between my heart and hand,
'Tween think-a-thing and do-another.

Never seen that neither. Don' matter.
It's there.
An' I pull, Lord Jesus Christ, sheets
Up over my face in the yellow night
An' hide, do hide – I curl to close the gap but can't.

But, clutch my heart – didn't I laugh love
At the smooth curve of her nostril?
Oh, that black rim swelled when she saw me close!
I opened her nose, did I,
And think-a-thing was spill myself in raindrops
    all around her.

But do-another was that when she couldn't
Look me plain and shining in the eye,
Or talk, or say my name but through the tooth,
Bitin' it, chewin', cain't swallow it down –
Was that even when my heart kept
Murmurin' *Baby, baby, I do love you,*
My hand, hard's a shoe heel,
Hit that nose cross-wise,
Cracked that faucet,
An' the blood poured out,

An' I caught that blood
(Lord Jesus!)
In my hand and
Hurled it crosst her face,
A stripe from eye to ear—
But what I heard, like my own mama murmurin',
Rockin' peaceful in a patterned quilt was
Baby, baby, baby, how I love you.

Palindromic: D.O.A. – O.D.

This hand, black as the Preacher's roll
An' thick as the thump of thunder,
Ain' got no handle for to hol';
    My Lord, it ain't no wonder—

This arm, this piston shaf' what drive
The wheel both up and under,
Broke on a pink slip—forty-five,
    'Tain't old, and ain't no wonder—

This man, he raised his face in rain
An' roared his manhood hunger.
This man done kilt hisself, a shame—
Bec at his belly, ice in his brain—
    Naw, Lord, it ain't no wonder.

Not Gently

Snow begins to grow on trees, to show
The willow's small bones white, while still some leaves
Persist in whispered conversation; snow

Begins to hush their rustling, and although
The sound be said in white the breathing trees
Must hold their speech, must mute the small *Hello*

They've murmured candle-wise to me. Now I know
There's some necessity in all of these
Divisions; I know that several years ago

The wide command included me, and I know
That laughter then held death against its knees –
But O my God, I will not let it go!

I cannot, cannot quit my walking now
When steps began in laughter; I cannot please
The silent snow nor mute the loud *Hello*

Demanded every step I take – and O
My God I will not let this sorrow freeze
The laughter which begot it. My God, I hold
These limbs in fury: I will not let them go!

Her Letter, Midwinter

I didn't think you'd come. There wasn't time
For you to drive so many miles from Wayne
In Canada to North Dakota. I'm—
I am content with that thought, as I was
Content when things were set for you to come. . . .

It's a pretty question, which is your home,
Isn't it?—whether it's the bedroom I
Have furnished with a length-wise love for you,
Or whether it is the necessity
Which rugs that other room so north of me?
Neither one, I suppose, since there are two.
You're called upon to be just where you are;
And you are thought upon not being here. . . .

I knew you couldn't come. You warned me, dear.
You said a thousand obligations try
If you can't go a little bit insane.
You said your mother carries a rouged death
Beneath her eyes, and deeper still a scar,
And you are her son. You warned me, and as
I live, I knew these things demanded you:
"Mother has clutched her terminus"—ah!—*"shawled
A piece of death around her shoulders—"* Who
Could have turned away from what was tenuous

To what was sure?—her ghostly, wintry breath
Against the life devoted, here, to us?
I knew these things. I knew. I knew. I knew—

But, Michael—you.
Might have called.

The Great Northern Between Towns

The steam-engine vomits for hating me
So much;
From Williston it curses me in its approach;
I *do* turn away, but it demands me crying by,
Flattens my dress against my thigh,
Gingham, cinder-spit, and sky—
And then, when it is gone,
Leaves me like a swatch of memory
Quickly forgot—
    Oh, God, but I
Am half afraid to be left this alone.

DE DOCTRINA CHRISTIANA, 2.6.7–8: A Terrifying Figure

Augustine thought he saw similitude
Between the "teeth" of the swart woman in
The Song of Songs, and ancient Saints: Saints chewed,
He said, "like teeth, the hardest hearts of men,"
Biting and shearing sinners from their errors—

My heart! My heart! Marge Piercy knows the truth:
They're tombstones. Teeth are the files of ice that chew
Me on a cold night, grinding me with terrors!

Austin said the sinner, softened, was gulped,
Then, to the body of the Church. He smiled—
A pleasant simile—
                    No! I am whipped,
Lashed by cords of snow that come snaking wild
Across the night fields to fix their fangs in
My face. This is no simile! Snow bites.
Cold bites. Ice bites, and swallows all I've been
Or would be, in an instant in the night.

Seminary Ridge, Gettysburg — January

Little trees—
Little trees—
Cry in the name of the Lord:
    You have no leaves.

Spindle trees—
Wooden knees,
Bend at the name of the Lord
    Good votaries—

Won't he weave
For who plead
Sweetly the name of the Lord
    Green seemly leaves?

Cold, mute trees! . . .
What are these?—
This wood, this whited chord
    The snowbird sees?

"Standing spears.
Soldiers' tears.
Arrowing prayers to the Lord
    That caught right here."

Little trees!
Little needs
Left since a wintering Lord
Webbed death for these.

Brittle trees,
I, sweet trees,
Grieve. In the name of the Lord,
You have no leaves—

Old Man, Out at Night

It took no companion to tell me why
Snow-devils hissed at me as I walked by,
And why the telephone wires said, *Lorn, lorn,*
And why the drifts had risen six feet high,
And why my God was laughing me to scorn—

Old Man, Remembering Children Deceased

When snowflakes fall into the lake
I like to think that they
Have slipped straight
Through.
Ah, it's not true.
But when they're hardened, say,
To hail, they'll float for anger's sake.

Mere Oblivion

Grey dawn, a winter's dawn. Snow—catatonic, vastly grey.
Two figures rise: a hawthorn trying painfully to pray,

An old man whose boot-toes are muzzles in the slow snow.
His beard is rimed; his eye has cross-hairs like a telescope;

He's keeping Candlemas but not in temples nor in thought:
This hunter plans to pierce mid-winter with one shot, one shot.

And so it happens. When in greylight he descries a hare,
He finds her eye—then cracks the dawn and lays his bullet there.

Mark that shot: a short distemper shakes the hare, brief and less
Than thinking: she grooms her head, kicks sidewards, and
    perishes.

No bone was broken; rather, two eyes have been soldered out.
One shot: the vermin died before the vermin had to doubt.

Hawthorn, this is the way the hunter prays the greydawn
    underneath.
Christian, this is his covenant with yet another marksman:
    Death.

IN MEAM COMMEMORATIONEM

I look for something solid in
The having been.
If it was once a fact
That I was young,
Then, though my youth
Has been displaced with a presuming age,
This nonetheless remains the truth,
That years and years ago
I was young. I seize that. I cage
It like a living nightingale.
I make what has been be.
And whatever else is wrong,
Whatever else has cracked
My faith like an impatient piece of glass,
I remember this:
Whatever is,
This was,
He was in love with me.

Winter's End in Storm

Leaves expectant; heavy bees
Drone in an air devoid of breeze
And, overall, expectant leaves.
　　I wait for rain as for a sneeze—

Lightning tickles; tangled trees
Are heaven's slightly crooked knees
Arrested darkly. Listen, leaves!
　　Thunder will be a mighty sneeze.

My wife will have to clear the lot
Of all the laundry, like as not.
　　And I'll get mud-sucked, like as not.
　　　Like as not.

Dust

I yearn
To curl in the corner
Of death's eye: Death's deep eye.
When he blinks
I am enclosed,
And I am washed
With weeping.

ET IN PACEM

Sitting and watching
The snow last night, Grandfather
Grinned. He has one tooth.

THE CHRIST MASS:

Back Through Headlong Time

I (strophe)

How did they kill the coyote?
They hardly knew.

They chased him, they raced him in exhaustless
Belly-treaded snowmobiles,
Snaring space on the open fields,
Stitching his tracks, exhausting him.

Wind in their beards, laughter cracking their teeth,
The sun a silver bugling on the snows,
They sliced the sound, they rode the brightness
Like tears on mirrors, exhausting him.

He squirt forward between their flanking,
Snapped tail to corner from a looping pincer,
Squeezed speed from his ribs—ran, ran,
His tongue blown backward at the ear.

How did they kill the coyote?
They never knew

That when they rode their mechanical rattlers
To the horizon, the coyote crack-plunged
Through the nooning crust
Of old spring snow—five feet in a white pit.

Exhausted, he could not leap nor dig long
Nor wait a better day or nourishment
But lay down in a lather, dying,
Till the foam was frozen on his shoulder.

How did they kill the coyote?
Like a roach in a teacup.

(antistrophe)

Jesus was born with hair
  With needle teeth
  A milk-blue breath
Four paws walking and aware:
A natal song we sing for thee;
In terra canunt angeli.

Mary his mother licked
  All lovingly
  His rheumy eye
With a doting tongue and quick:
And lullabies we croon to thee;
In terra canunt angeli.

Flesh of the flesh of beasts
  Creation's ward
  Who was its Lord
Born to host, to meat our feasts:
Astonished hymns and litanies
In terra canunt angeli.

Cub of Creation, go
  Break from thy den
  Run among men
Cross our Colorado snows—
And prove what sort of beasts we be.
In terra canunt angeli,
Et lamentantur archangeli.

II *(strophe)*

And the wolf—
How did they kill the wolf?
Slit a salt-lick
Grind a deep groove
Etch a sheath: slip
The blade within
This sheath edge-up
And pack the crack.

But the wolf—
How did they kill the wolf?
He ran his tongue
Like a muslin
Of flesh across
The salt: drool from
Joints in his jaw
Numbed the tongue-cuts.

How did they kill the wolf?
His drooling dropped
Blood: blood he lapped
Blood he hungered
Lord so fiercely
His stomach seized
At warm rich blood.

The wolf? The wolf—
Bled forth his food
Swallowed gulped and
Did not know he
Was his prey: he
Praised God that all
He wished he had.

Oh you blessèd
Block of Sweetblood!—
The wolf: he drained
And drank his life
By the self-same
Lacerated
Howling organ. . . .

Speak to me speak
To me speak to
Me how did they
Kill the wolf? *Did*
They kill the wolf?
Did he know he
Craved his own blood?

(antistrophe)

Mary delivered Jesus on her knees,
Pushed him head-downward to the scalloped earth
Bare between her knees, pressed for all her worth
With both hands folded on her belly, squeezed
Her lids and lips, her teeth, her being (*Please*)
To drive him down, to bring him to his birth;
Mary (*God! God! Father of this hard hurt,*
Please! Let your baby come!) begged on her knees—

And this is how God solved her maidenhood:
She tore.
In a rush the flesh burst like a breached door,
Blood poured
Before and with and on the infant. Blood:
His first milk, air, his swaddling—and all his mother's good.

III (strophe)

But even the cow was aided in her birthing.
"Y'hear that woofing?" Edward said. "She's choked
At the wrong end. Wear my boots." And we went.

Since she'd been laboring, lowing all night long,
To bring her calf breech-wise into the world,
Edward tied a cord around the soft hooves
That stuck out beneath her tail like tails,
And tugged. Her sides heaved. He put a foot
To her hips to help himself and tugged
Till they sweat together, the calf between.
"Let go let go let go"– But who was holding?

The sun breached the horizon. Fog crawled the fields
Burning. Me, I took her blameless gaze.

As though the calf suddenly gave up haven,
It plunged out and Edward sat backward
With a slick busybody bumping for footing,
Immediately, on his impossible pants.

But what I recall with dazzled gratitude
Seeing, was the balloon of fluid that followed
This calf into the world, a globe no one had promised.
Morning sunlight fused in it and set it glowing,
Till Edward took his thick farmer's finger
And stabbed the bladder, collapsing it – and
Its heavy water washed the earth. Amen.

(antistrophe)

There came a moment when
Resting on her pallet
　　Mary sat upright
As though remembering,
As though she'd say, "I know—
　　I know it now."

But she held her peace, did Mary.
A smile like blotted water
　　Darkened her mouth,
Like a new rain freshet,
Spilled on the ledges below
　　Her eyes: *I know—*

She bowed her head sideways
As though she were listening
　　To a word at her vulva.
Does melting make a sound?
Her hair spilled all on her
　　Left breast: *I know—*

Then she touched the man beside her
Lightly, to leave the moment
　　Undisturbed,
And whispered like a spray
Of roses, roses: "Joseph,
　　My water broke."

IV (strophe)

Who teaches developing girls to tread
Ground preciously, with a faint step, as though
Hobbled by dread or by great sympathy?
When do they learn the earth is their sister? . . .

Did you, the old man peered, *swaller that seed?*
His grandchild paused, her face lost in a smile
Of watermelon rind, frowning because
She trusted his decrees as trust a priest.

Swaller a seed, he said, *your tummy swells
And soon you have a baby, Fi-fo-fum!*
—A young girl, greatly burdened, went to walk
The cornfields, to pray God about a seed.

Illinois soil is black as blankets. She
Paused at a corn crib. Grandpa, his hands tucked
Under the bib of his overalls, gross
Contentment, came, and gazed away from her.

Illinois evening skies are amethyst;
Corduroy cornfields float below from here
To the horizon, irrigated with
A running darkness down the rows. Black blood.

You worried? Grandpa wondered of the west-
Northwest. His grandchild did not nod, but frowned.
'Cause eatin' seeds, he said, *naw— 'tain't no bane.
Earth ate a load o' seed, an' look at her.*

Look at her swell—green an' so pretty, child,
I want to cry. She's pregnant, don't you know.
I hear this earth o' mine, hear the black dirt
Low, like a mama moanin' nursery rhymes.

Illinois cornfields form a church of pews;
Grandpa, slouching at the corn crib as priests
Slouch twice the Verba, had an acolyte
Beside him, lighting candles in her eyes.

All them seedlings is her litter, he said,
Her babies, curled and yearnin' to the birth.
Listen: can't you hear the blood rush, and deep
Roots suckin' nourishment? she heard. She learned—

That she stood on the holy woman, Earth,
Stood on a great womb fat to teeming young.
In that night she learned to walk as women
Do: soft, cautiously, barely brushing ground.

Come fall, Fi-fo-fum, Grandpa winked, *come fall,*
He said, *we'll grind her corn to make our bread.*
—That night engendered in a girlchild love
And a deep dread, both, for Earth and for her
Self, forever.

(antistrophe)

Jesus was strong, strong as the storm;
He churned the waters ere he was born.

Jesus was merry, imp of the sun;
He caused the waters to giggle and run.

He raised a wave that slapped the shore
Not after birth—a month before!

O mother of our infant king,
How *did* he such a marvelous thing?

(And Mary remembers the full-some days
With shining eyes and quiet praise)

While I bathed naked in the lake
He kicked, for all creation's sake.

My belly punched out willfully:
'Twas him in a hurry, none but he.

Oh, mine was a monstrous pod to bear,
Lord of the seas, the land, and air:

But while he lingered in his daughter
I was the weather that dashed the water;

I was a planet, God's low girl,
A green, complete, and turning world.

    Earth! Sweet earth!
    With love we burst.

V (strophe)

In the zygote seed
All we need.

Parts die:
Male and female
In travail;
Natures human and divine
Still perishing
Till IS is one one satisfies
And all is me
But none am I
Since AM is pure divinity.

The zygote cell:
Emmanuel,
Being indivisible.

Tell me why,
In the first spring rain,
Do they cry
And the fields hiss pain?
It's we, sweet Jesus, we—
The grain deceased in thee.

(antistrophe)

When Gabriel departed and all glory,
And water was bubbling, and I remembered the coals
I'd blown before the angel stood before me;

When I knelt down with tongs to spread those coals—
My left hand on my thigh, my right hand reaching—
Hardly recalling bright news for clay bowls;

When someone sang "Mary?" in the courtyard, each thing
Common in my lot, equable as sand,
Then, just then, I felt—I call it a "stitching"

In my right side, low down and deep. *Stand! Stand
Up, Mary,* I thought; but I could not move.
This ache in my pelvis, this light larval spasm—

I, who had never known motion in the caves of
My womanhood, cried: "The egg—drops! Oh, my love!"

Reprise

Christmas and his Incarnation,
Dimpled time, time in a vortex,
Time sucked backward through itself, and
We return through its forward going:
We, by mercy, pass its latter sadness first; we
Meet its middle as our own, most penitential;
We arrive then at its first, the simplex,
Our last home and holing.

This is the marvel of our celebration
And the grace of God:
To take us back
Through headlong time,
To make us small
And tuck us home
Again.

O baby, rest your nappy head;
Your eyes be rollin', you half dead;
Your mama loves you, wide and deep—
O baby, baby, get some sleep:
  Your story's done
    Begun.

EPILOGUE

(An Apologia)

Harlequin, Finding His Voice

I'll give my poetry the kind
Of strictures Jonson gave his mind
And give my mind the freedom he
Would give his poetry.

Then, if the thought *is* dead for all
The centuries of dying it
Had undergone before I called
It out of my young wit,

A dizzy erudition in
The way I say the thing may win
It life again and something new
For telling it to you.

Our busy-ness is to invert
The funnel masters used, to blurt
A little thought as if we had
A trumpet and were mad.

Some Lines of Criticism:
The Barkeep Speaks

"High Sentence," Bailey said, "and Solace too."
But solace was a British cockatoo;
Solace was gentle Nicholas and Alison,
A willing kiss, a warm return, and Absolon.
And solace, now I come to think of it,
Was all that tickled Harry Bailey's wit.
Great Bailey! He's the people's critic now,
And all the pain the censors will allow,
That's solace. Sentence, please you, 's been reduced
To subject, verb, objection, and abuse.

Regarding Confessional Poets: The Fusion

The trouble with atomic bombs
Is lethal egocentricity:
When one remarks upon himself
There goes the near vicinity.

Whereas, Decorum . . .

i.
In the waving of
Tall grass, and its wet smiling,
Lo! a little man.

ii.
Listen. The dry leaves
Are children chasing me to
Skip in my stories.

Poet, Venator

A fox is always a thing running-gone.
Too bad. I'd like her still to think upon.
But we're the ones who cut her from the brush
And said that that's to rest but she's to rush,
Or be rushed, or be running—as you will.
We couldn't think on something standing still.
Not us. If God himself begins to run
(Why not? Grant God an interstellar fun)
We'll after him, intent upon the kill.
Anything. We'll chase anything up-hill.

The Temple and the Miniature: Mosquitoes

They die so easily, these little things;
Flying thread-knots, they've got pine-sliver limbs
And tiny, tiny gardens for eyes. They're
Constructed of bitterness and accident,
You know—every last one of them; so they share
With us the consequence of that moment when God
Would share just nothing with us. You sing your hymns,
Herbert, and I'll sing mine; and the one who sings
Encomiums to a mosquito sings
To that thing where God is not but in spent
Anger. You praise his Presence, George; I'll prod
Around and rummage in his Absence. Between
Us we ought to strike some order on the earth.
You kill, I'll mourn the little creature's little spleen
And look for her to dawdle through a second birth.
George Herbert, we'll get on—and God, then, will have been.

To God My God in My Extremities

When I diffuse beyond my self and lose
The sane, good grasp upon my second soul;
When nature can no longer meet her whole
Revolvement here in me, proving the ruse
Of winter, as she used to do, by my
Joy in the sweet spring steaming from the trees
(The joy was once her closure); when I please
Some black bewilderment, and a storm sky
Founders the understanding of my heart—
Then I return to poetry, and by
Its straights, its patterns and its narrows, I
Return to you: I prove your love. My art
Has found no firmer ground than this, that you
Love me; and I have found no course more true.

My Verses, My Obedience

—Because, sir, the ability
To will and then to do belongs
To God; and nothing else I know
(A branch divides upon its tree,
The thrush is busy with her songs,
Sir, when she will) is peace below—